50 THINGS TO KNOW

BOOK SERIES
REVIEWS FROM READERS

I recently downloaded a couple of books from this series to read over the weekend thinking I would read just one or two. However, I so loved the books that I read all the six books I had downloaded in one go and ended up downloading a few more today. Written by different authors, the books offer practical advice on how you can perform or achieve certain goals in life, which in this case is how to have a better life.

The information is simple to digest and learn from, and is incredibly useful. There are also resources listed at the end of the book that you can use to get more information.

50 Things To Know To Have A Better Life: Self-Improvement Made Easy!

Author Dannii Cohen

This book is very helpful and provides simple tips on how to improve your everyday life. I found it to be useful in improving my overall attitude.

50 Things to Know For Your Mindfulness & Meditation Journey
Author Nina Edmondso

Quick read with 50 short and easy tips for what to think about before starting to homeschool.

50 Things to Know About Getting Started with Homeschool by Author Amanda Walton

I really enjoyed the voice of the narrator, she speaks in a soothing tone. The book is a really great reminder of things we might have known we could do during stressful times, but forgot over the years.

Author Harmony Hawaii

There is so much waste in our society today. Everyone should be forced to read this book. I know I am passing it on to my family.

50 Things to Know to Downsize Your Life: How To Downsize, Organize, And Get Back to Basics

Author Lisa Rusczyk Ed. D.

Great book to get you motivated and understand why you may be losing motivation. Great for that person who wants to start getting healthy, or just for you when you need motivation while having an established workout routine.

50 Things To Know To Stick With A Workout: Motivational Tips To Start The New You Today

Author Sarah Hughes

50 THINGS TO KNOW ABOUT MARS

Facts and Trivia About the Red Planet

R. Vincent

Cover designed by: Ivana Stamenkovic
Cover Image: https://pixabay.com/photos/mars-red-planet-
planet-space-11012/

CZYK Publishing Since 2011.
CZYKPublishing.com
50 Things to Know

Lock Haven, PA
ISBN: 9798738711541

50 THINGS TO KNOW ABOUT MARS

BOOK DESCRIPTION

Why is Mars red? Is there life on Mars? Will humans ever set foot on Mars? If you have asked any of these questions, this book is for you.

50 Things to Know About Mars by R. Vincent offers a fun, informative, and accessible approach to answering some of the most common questions about Mars. This book presents interesting facts about Mars without getting too boring and technical.

In these pages you'll discover information about the history of Mars and its features. You'll be able to compare Mars to other planets in the solar system, including our own. You'll learn about past, present, and future missions to Mars and what's been learned from them so far. You'll understand how human perception of Mars has changed over the years and how important the planet may be to our future. So, grab YOUR copy today. You'll be glad you did.

TABLE OF CONTENTS

DEDICATION

This book is dedicated to the memories of the men and women who have lost their lives in the pursuit of greater understanding of our universe through space travel.

ABOUT THE AUTHOR

R. Vincent is a former engineer and physics professor.

He is currently a freelance author on various subjects with an emphasis on science and technology.

INTRODUCTION

"Space… is big. Really big. You
just won't believe how vastly hugely
mind-bogglingly big it is. I mean,
you may think it's a long way down
the road to the chemist, but that's
just peanuts to space."

- Douglas Adams

S ince ancient times, people have been looking up at the night sky, fascinated by all the brilliant points of light. Most of those lights – the stars and galaxies – seemed to always be in the same position relative to each other in the sky. They were so stationary that they could be used for orientation and navigation, and we've been seeing the same star constellations for millennia. But there were a few oddballs that moved around in strange patterns. They appeared to slowly zigzag in curved, arcing paths across the sky.

The ancient Greeks called these meandering stars "planetes", or "the wanderers". But it turned out that they weren't stars at all. Later, astronomers figured out that these strange bodies were not giving off their own light like faraway stars, but rather were revolving in orbits around the Sun, reflecting its light to our eyes. They were planets, just like the Earth.

Our Sun is just over four light years, or about 25 trillion miles, away from the next closest star system. With the fastest spacecraft humans have ever built to date, it would take about 18,000 years to make that journey. Fortunately, there are much closer celestial neighbors to visit. With seven other planets (plus the recently demoted dwarf planet Pluto) and dozens of moons in our own solar system, there's more than enough to explore.

Understanding other planets helps us understand our own planet, our cosmological history, and our place in the universe. Mars is interesting because it is like Earth in many respects and is a close orbital neighbor. Mars has inspired scientists, engineers, authors, and movie makers over the years because it is so close and accessible.

Humans are too restless and curious to remain on Earth forever, and in the future, if our planet is ever in peril, Mars could be the next logical place to call home.

1. MARS – FOURTH ROCK FROM THE SUN

The solar system consists of the Sun and the eight planets (in order from the Sun out) Mercury, Venus, Earth, Mars, Jupiter, Saturn, Uranus, and Neptune. There are also many moons, an asteroid belt, and several other smaller bodies like comets and some "dwarf" planets (like Pluto). Mars is the fourth closest planet to the Sun, and Earth's astronomical next-door neighbor.

Although Venus is closest in size to Earth, and slightly closer in orbit, it is very different from Earth. It has a thick, sulfurous, poisonous atmosphere and is extremely hot due to being so close to the Sun, so it's not an ideal place to visit.

Mars, on the other hand, is much cooler and has a less dangerous atmosphere than Venus. Compared to Earth, it has the most similarities. It has some water, mostly in the form of ice, and a relatively dormant landscape. These features have made Mars the most studied planet in the solar system other than Earth, and the next destination for human explorers after the Moon.

2. THE RED PLANET

Of all the stars, planets, and galaxies that are visible in the sky, there has always been something very peculiar about Mars. Even when seen without the aid of a telescope, Mars has a very distinctive reddish hue. We understand now that the iconic red color of Mars is owed to the oxidized iron (essentially, rust) on its surface, but our ancestors had a much more poetic explanation.

The ancient Romans seemed to always be at war. They had a huge army made of multiple battalions, fighting in faraway territories all over the empire. The Roman god Mars (who was equivalent to the Greek god Ares), was therefore very important to Rome because he was the god of war.

Ancient peoples often paired their gods with bodies in the heavens, like the Sun, the stars, planets, and moons. The Romans were no exception. For example, Jupiter, the largest planet in our solar system, was named after the chief Roman god of the same name. The unique blood red color of the planet Mars was similarly associated with the war god Mars.

3. THE "TWIN" MOONS

Although Mars has always been visible to human observers, it wasn't until the late 19th century that we learned it had two tiny satellites in orbit around it. In 1877, American astronomer Asaph Hall discovered the existence of the two oddly shaped rocky moons.

The moons of mars once again owe their names to the Greek and Roman pantheon of gods. Ares, the Greek equivalent of the Roman god Mars, was said to have two sons - Phobos (meaning "fear") and Deimos (meaning "dread") - whose names were given to the moons.

Phobos in Deimos are both very small compared to most moons in the solar system, especially that of Earth. Phobos is less than 14 miles across (about the size of the island of Manhattan!), while Deimos is less than 8 miles long. Since they are so small, they don't have enough mass for gravitational forces to form them into spherical shapes, so they are often described as looking like giant potatoes.

While the origin of the moons is unclear, scientists speculate that they may have been wayward asteroids passing by and captured by Mars' gravity.

4. PHOBOS: CHASING THE MOON

The largest of Mars' twin moons, Phobos, also has the shallowest orbit of the two bodies. Phobos, in fact, has the shallowest orbit of any known moon in the solar system. Because of its low orbit, Phobos revolves very fast around its host planet.

Moons tend to orbit their planets in the same direction as the planet's rotation, but most moons complete one revolution in a shorter time than the planet completes a rotation. This is why a moon will appear to rise in one direction of the sky and set in the other.

Phobos, however, revolves faster than a Martian day – much faster. So, it doesn't lag behind the rotation of Mars. Phobos is so fast that it passes through the visible sky twice a day and it appears to rise and move in the opposite direction as its slower twin Deimos, even though they both orbit in the same direction.

5. MARS OF THE PAST

The planets of our solar system (or any solar system) haven't always been like they are now. A couple of billion years ago the Earth was just a dry, lifeless rock. Now the Earth is covered in a vast ocean. It turns out that Earth and Mars may have reversed roles, to an extent, over the eons since our system formed.

We see Mars now as a dry, cold, dusty wasteland with few interesting features other than craters and rocks. But if you look closer, you see evidence of dried-up lake beds, eroded river valleys, and even deltas. There is strong evidence that during several periods in its distant past liquid water could have existed on the surface of Mars.

We know there is some water locked up as ice near its polar regions, but it's not clear how much. There is also a small amount of water vapor in the Martian atmosphere. So, the water is there, making the idea of a warmer, wetter Mars of the past plausible. Geological studies suggest that the surface temperature of Mars cooled over time, freezing most of its water.

6. IRON AND THE RED PLANET

Mars is famous for its rusty red color. It is, after all, called the "Red Planet" for a reason. When it is visible in the sky, it can even be distinguished from other stars and planets with the naked eye due its red tint. The reason for this distinct coloration is that almost its entire visible surface is covered with a dust layer composed of iron oxide.

When certain metals come into contact with oxygen atoms (with help of a catalyst like water) they tend to oxidize to form a new compound. We see this when water gets on iron-based metals like steel and makes rust. The iron that is part of the structure of Mars was somehow exposed to water and oxygen during its formation. Pure iron forms iron oxide after oxidation, which has the familiar dark red rusty color.

It's interesting to note that Mars was named after the Roman god of war due to its "bloody" appearance. The same substance, iron oxide, that gives Mars its famous color is what makes blood red as well.

7. ANATOMY OF A PLANET

We don't know as much about the interior of Mars as we do about the Earth, but various scientific studies and some educated guesses can paint a plausible picture of its composition.

The inner core of Mars is dense and likely composed primarily of solid metal like many rocky planets. Iron and nickel will make up most of the core, and there is probably a large amount of sulfer as well. Outside Mars' solid core is a softer mantle made of molten and rocky material including iron, silicon, and oxygen.

The crust is largely iron, the surface of which has been oxidized by previous exposure to oxygen and water. There are also other metals and minerals in the crust like aluminum and magnesium. Colder regions of Mars, especially near the poles, have frozen carbon dioxide (dry ice) and water ice, some of which exist just below the surface.

8. TALE OF THE TAPE: EARTH VS. MARS

Mars is the planet in our solar system that is most like Earth. It has a similar rocky composition, and is the next planet from the Sun, making it a close neighbor. How does Mars measure up to Earth?

Mars is just over half the diameter of Earth. The Earth's diameter at the equator (no planet is a perfect sphere, they "bulge" at the equator) is 12,750 km, or about 7920 miles. Mars is 6790 km at its equator, or about 4220 miles. These numbers translate into a circumference of 40,075 km (24,900 miles) for Earth and 21,344 km (13,260 miles) for Mars.

So, we know Earth has a hefty waistline compared to Mars, but how to they weigh in? You'd think that if Mars was half the diameter of Earth it would be about half its mass, but that's not the case. Because of the geometry of spheres and differing compositions, Mars' mass is about 6.4×10^{23} kg, about a tenth of the Earth's mass.

9. GRAVITY ON MARS

The law of gravity says that any two objects with mass will be attracted to one another, and that attraction is greater with greater masses (it's also less the further apart the objects are). So, the greater the mass of a planet, the more it attracts the objects near its surface.

Gravity is most often measured by the acceleration produced in masses because of the attraction. On Earth, that acceleration is about 9.8 meters per square second (m/s^2) or 32 ft/s^2. Since Mars is smaller than Earth and has a somewhat different composition, its mass and diameter give it a different gravitational pull. Acceleration due to gravity on Mars is only about 3.7 m/s^2 near the surface – about 38% of Earth's gravity.

This means that a 150 lb. person walking on the surface of Mars would feel like they only weigh about 57 lbs. Don't get too excited though… it may seem like a great weight loss plan, but your correct weight will be right where it started back on Earth!

10. MARTIAN GEOGRAPHY 101

Although Mars is not separated into oceans and continents like the Earth, it is still useful to divide it into contiguous regions to help locate different surface features and study variations in its landscape. It's also useful to have a standard reference map of the planet's surface for planning missions that use landers and rovers.

Like the Earth, Mars is divided into latitude and longitude lines to provide 2-dimensional coordinates for any point on its surface. Thus, it features identified north and south poles, an equator, and a prime meridian. Elevations have been mapped by orbital surveys of the planet.

Additionally, the surface is divided into 30 patches or "quadrangles" with unique names. These areas include the north and south poles, 16 regions lining the equator, and 12 regions in the intermediate areas. Within these regions are individual named features like mountains, valleys, craters, canyons, troughs, and plains.

11. CRATERS ON MARS

Mars, like the other planets and moons in our solar system, has been bombarded with space debris throughout its history. When asteroids or meteors crash into a planet (often accompanied by a large explosion), the impact leaves an indentation in the form of a crater.

Like the Moon, Mars' surface is pockmarked with multiple craters (hundreds of thousands), many of which have been there for many millions of years. Because Mars has a relatively thin atmosphere, more meteors make it to the surface than they do on Earth. Also, since it has a very inactive crust, the resulting craters remain indefinitely.

Many of the larger or more interesting craters on Mars have been given names. The largest is the Huygens crater, which is about 290 miles across. Some craters are destinations for study by current and future landing missions.

12. OLYMPUS MONS

The Earth has a very active crust and has approximately 1,500 volcanoes, many of which are still active. The largest volcano on Earth is Mauna Loa on the island of Hawaii, standing over 9 km high. You may be surprised to learn, however, that the largest volcano in the solar system is on the planet Mars.

Unlike Earth, Mars only has 20 volcanoes and none of them are currently active, but it does have bragging rights for the largest volcano of all the planets in our system with the enormous Olympus Mons. Olympus Mons stands at 21 km - far taller than any volcano or mountain on Earth.

Olympus Mons is a "shield volcano", meaning it has a wide, flat shape. So, in addition to being very tall, it covers a large area of ground. The total cone of the volcano covers an area that is roughly the size of the country of France.

Olympus Mons means Mt. Olympus, named for the mythic home of the ancient Greek gods.

13. THE MARTIAN ATMOSPHERE

There are two main features that characterize a planet's (or moon's) atmosphere – chemical composition and atmospheric pressure. The Earth's atmosphere is composed of 78% nitrogen and 19% oxygen, with the remaining portion consisting of trace amounts of various other gases. The sea-level pressure is about 15 lbs. per square inch. Our moon has no atmospheric gases and is surrounded by a vacuum (zero pressure).

The Martian atmosphere, by contrast, is mostly carbon dioxide – over 95% and contains only 1% oxygen, making it unbreathable for humans. There rest is composed of nitrogen, argon, and some trace gases.

Mars' atmosphere is also much thinner than Earth's, but not like the vacuum of the moon. The atmospheric pressure on Mars less than one tenth of one pound per square inch near the ground. Despite its thin air, Mars has considerable wind and dust storms throughout the planet.

14. MARTIAN WEATHER

"Good morning, everybody! It's going to be a brisk negative 55 degrees today with a 20 mile-per-hour breeze out of the northeast, so be sure to grab your jackets. And watch out for dust storms!"

How would you like to wake up to the radio in the morning and hear the weather report above? That's about what you'd expect on a typical day on the planet Mars.

Like Earth, Mars has a tilt to its axis of rotation, so it has some seasonal variations in climate between its northern and southern hemispheres. However, the Earth's vast ocean has a significant impact on regulating temperature. Mars is much drier and further from the Sun than Earth, so its weather patterns are very different than Earth's.

An average temperature of −63 °C (−81 °F) is common on Mars. Extremes can range from a low of −153 °C (−243 °F) in the polar regions to a high of 20 °C (68 °F) closer to the equator. Recorded winds have ranged from 20 to 30 mph, with gusts up to 60 mph during the dust storms which are common on the planet.

15. THE SUN AND SKY FROM MARS

Sunrises and sunsets can be some of the most spectacular sights on Earth. The low angle of the sun in the sky can produce a kaleidoscope of color. But what would a sunset look like on Mars?

Mars is about 50 percent further from the Sun than the Earth is. As a result, the size of the Sun as it appears in the Martian sky is roughly two thirds the size that it appears to us. The Sun also only appears about 40% as bright on Mars as it does on Earth.

The combination of sunlight and the dusty red atmosphere of Mars make for an interesting daytime sky in clear conditions. On normal, clear days the Martian sky appears light red – almost pink. But on "cloudy" days, when water vapor forms tiny ice crystals, a dark violet color appears.

Interestingly, during sunrise and sunset on Mars, the sky in the vicinity of the Sun appears blue like the daytime sky on Earth.

16. ORBIT

When our solar system began to form some 4.5 Billion years ago, our young Sun was surrounded by a spinning disc of dust and gas. Over time, gravitational forces caused larger and larger clumps of material to form at various distances from the Sun. These clumps continued to grow until each became a planet.

The planets continue to revolve in the direction of that original disc, but each in their own orbit. Although orbits appear to be circular paths, they are actually ellipses, so they are closer to the Sun at different points in their orbits.

The Earth's orbit is, on average, 93 million miles from the Sun, which has been defined as 1 Astronomical Unit (AU). Mars sits at 1.5 AU, or nearly 140 million miles from the Sun. Mars and Earth pass closest to each other about every two years, but the minimum distance between the planets changes due to their elliptical orbits.

17. THE MARTIAN CALENDAR: LONG DAYS AND LONGER YEARS

A day is the time it takes a planet to make one complete rotation on its axis. On Earth that takes exactly 24 of our hours – because we have defined one hour as 1/24th of a day. The rotation speed of Mars is similar to that of Earth, but slightly slower. Using Earth hours, it takes Mars approximately 24 hours 40 minutes to make one rotation. We call days on other planets "sols", short for solar days.

A year is the time it takes a planet to make one complete revolution around the Sun. Because Mars is further from the Sun than Earth is, it has a much longer orbital path to take and thus its year is also longer. A Martian year is about 669 Mars sols which comes out to about 687 Earth days - nearly two Earth years!

So, future Mars colonists will only be able to celebrate their birthday every two years – but at least they'll get an extra 40 minutes of sleep each day!

18. WATER ON MARS

Looking through a telescope, or at the increasing number of high-definition photographs sent back to Earth from space probes and Martian rovers, it's easy to view Mars as nothing but a red, barren desert. Water is not as abundant on Mars as it is on Earth, but Mars does have a surprising amount of water.

Water exists almost entirely in two forms on Mars. Most of it is locked up in ice and a much smaller amount exists in the Martian atmosphere in the form of water vapor. Much of the ice exists in the polar regions of Mars, both above and below the visible surface.

There doesn't seem to be much liquid water on the planet, but it occasionally appears in transition between ice and vapor. Although no rain has been observed on Mars, it does periodically get a very thin layer of frost on the surface. There are even some snowfalls, but much of the snow consists of dry ice (carbon dioxide) since there is only little water in the atmosphere.

19. MAGNETIC FIELD

Space is a dangerous place. Aside from the airless vacuum, it is permeated with a high level of radiation, mostly from the Sun's rays. One of the features that makes Earth a hospitable place for life is its magnetic field, which acts as a shield against most solar and cosmic radiation. The magnetic field is generated by the circular movement of molten iron and nickel in the Earth's core.

Mars, however, doesn't have a circulating core of magnetic material to make its own strong magnetic field. Geological studies show that it may have had such a field in the past, but that the metal core has since solidified. Mars does have a magnetic field because of the presence of metals, but it is comparatively weak.

Human visitors to Mars will need to use artificial shielding to protect themselves from radiation.

20. LIFE ON MARS?

The prospect of life on other planets is naturally fascinating to curious humans wondering if we are alone in the universe. The idea of finding life on Mars is even more tantalizing due to its proximity to Earth. When talking about life on Mars, though, we don't mean "little green men", or giant tentacled monsters hell-bent on invading Earth. Those ideas were put to rest when space probes discovered the desolation and atmospheric conditions of Mars.

Life, specifically microscopic and microbial life, has been found on Earth in environments that we previously thought impossible. Boiling and sulfurous volcanic ocean vents, ice, deep underground chasms, and the cold, dark seabed all support some kind of life. Although actual evidence of life, past or present, has yet to be found on Mars, studies of its composition and geological history suggest that it could have supported certain forms of life.

Mars contains some of the basic organic compounds that form the basis of life, liquid water was present at some point in its past. Current Mars missions are actively seeking more signs of life on our red neighbor - if they are found it would be one of the most important discoveries in human history.

21. PERCIVAL LOWELL AND THE MARTIAN CANALS

Percival Lowell was an American businessman and scientist who gained some notoriety in the late 1800's with his claims that Mars featured a system of water canals. Although a few astronomers in the 19th Century had previously claimed to observe canals, Lowell popularized the idea with several books on the topic.

The notion of canals on Mars fueled speculation and imagination in popular culture. Theories as to the origin and structure of the canals led to ideas that there could be living, intelligent creatures there. The concept of the "Martian" as a race of being was born and many works of science fiction referred to Martians and canals.

As telescopes improved in range and clarity, skeptical astronomers were able to show that the lines Lowell thought were canals were an optical illusion created by the heavily cratered surface of Mars. To be fair to Percival Lowell, he was a very accomplished well-respected astronomer, and even discovered the planet (now, dwarf planet) Pluto.

22. MARS IN LITERATURE

Books and stories about Mars date back to the 1600's, but ever since speculation about the presence of engineered canals in the late 19th century, more authors began using Mars as a backdrop for fantasy and fiction stories, both romantic and horrifying. Most of these early stories featured intelligent Martian beings that often reflected positive and negative human traits.

One of the most enduring early examples of Mars fiction was The War of the Worlds (1898) by the science fiction author H.G. Wells. The War of the Worlds depicted Martians as an advanced race of large squid-like creatures who invade Earth to exploit its resources. Later, Edgar Rice Burroughs penned a series of pulp-fiction stories about Mars that became the novel A Princess of Mars (1912) about a man from Earth who falls in love with a Martian Princess.

After space probes and landers from Earth revealed the desolate nature of Mars in the 1960's and 1970's, literature evolved to become more believably about Mars' future as a second home for Earthlings.

23. FACES AND PYRAMIDS ON MARS

Once space probes began photographing Mars up close, ideas about Martian beings and advanced civilizations were put to rest... but only temporarily.

When NASA's Viking mission was orbiting Mars in 1976 looking for a safe place to land, it sent several photographs of the Martian surface back to Earth. One photograph of a region of Mars called Cydonia featured several interesting rock formations. One of them had the unmistakable appearance of a sphinx-like human face – complete with eyes, nose, and mouth – looking up from the surface. Other rocks nearby had the appearance of large man-made pyramids.

These images resulted in 25 years of renewed speculation and conspiracy theories about lost or hidden Martian civilizations. But in 2001, high-definition images of the same region taken by the Mars Global Surveyor showed that the face and pyramid images were simply optical illusions created by shadows and image anomalies. People often see what they want to see!

24. MARS ATTACKS NEW JERSEY

When English science fiction writer H.G. Wells wrote his 1898 book The War of the Worlds, about a Martian invasion of Earth, it's unlikely that he could have anticipated the minor, but surreal, panic it would cause some 40 years later across the Atlantic.

The night before Halloween in 1938, radio and film star Orson Welles and other actors performed a dramatic reading on CBS Radio in New York of a fake news broadcast that described the events in The War of the Worlds as if they were happening in real time. The result was that several listeners were under the impression that they were hearing live reports of an alien attack on the town of Grover's Mill, New Jersey.

Several hours of chaos ensued, including visits from police and concerned citizens, until the radio station could convince everyone that giant Martian monsters were not ravaging the Garden State.

25. MARS ON SCREEN

Mars is unique among the planets of our solar system in its similarity and closeness to Earth, making it the best candidate for life and future human habitation. Speculation about Mars has captured the imaginations of moviegoers since the earliest days of cinema. Like literature, movies have reflected the state of understanding about the planet during their respective eras.

In the first half of the twentieth century, before the age of space exploration, it was still feasible in the minds of many that there could be living, intelligent beings, or "Martians" on the Red Planet. These counterparts to humans were given complex societies and technologies like in the Danish silent film A Trip to Mars (1918).

Mirroring changes in fiction literature about Mars, modern films concentrate more on humans and colonization. The popular film The Martian (2015), for example, depicted an abandoned astronaut trying to survive in a scientific station on Mars.

26. NASA AND MARS

The National Aeronautics and Space Administration (NASA) was established in 1958 by the US government as a civilian agency for space science and exploration. Advances in rocketry and pressure to keep up with Soviet space efforts drove NASA's missions to begin sending crafts and people into space.

While most of NASA's early efforts focused on Earth satellites, manned orbiters, and exploration of the moon, it sent several probes to Mars in the 1960's and 1970's – some in "flyby" missions and some orbiters. It even landed probes on Mars in the late 70's.

NASA then turned its attention to the space shuttle program and the International Space Station for a couple of decades before renewing missions in the 1990's with more orbiters, landers, and rovers. Now the agency is exploring plans to eventually send people to walk on the surface of Mars, perhaps by the 2030's.

27. JPL – THE ROCKET SPECIALISTS

Research and Development is essential to safe and productive space exploration. Originally established in the 1930's by the California Institute of Technology to study rocket engine technology, the Jet Propulsion Laboratory (JPL) is now federally funded to support NASA in its space exploration missions.

JPL has been involved in the development and execution of missions to Mars since the earliest US probes were launched in the 1960's, including the first flyby's, orbiters, and landers. It is now instrumental in the many recent and ongoing missions that have landed robotic rovers on the Martian surface that are providing valuable information about the planet.

Several NASA Mars missions are now controlled remotely from JPL's site in southern California.

28. GETTING TO MARS: IT'S ALL ABOUT TIMING

Traveling from Earth to Mars is not like going from L.A. to New York, or even like flying from the Earth to the Moon, where the distance traveled is always essentially the same. Since Earth and Mars are on different orbital paths, they are both constantly moving with respect to each other.

At its closest distance to Earth, every two years, Mars is usually between about 35 and 65 million miles from Earth. That big variation is due to their elliptical orbits. At its furthest, Mars can be over 250 million miles from Earth, and that doesn't even account for the fact that you would have to go around the Sun to get there!

When sending a rocket to Mars, then, the timing is usually selected to take advantage of the Mars' closest approach to Earth. If leaving at the right time, rockets can "meet" Mars at its closest point. Modern rockets can typically make the one-way trip in about seven months.

29. MARS COMMUNICATION

The speed of light is fast - very fast. In fact, it's the fastest thing we know of. In free space, light travels nearly 300 million meters, or about 186,000 miles, per second. Over short distances that seems instantaneous to us, but over the vast distances of space it takes time to get from one place to another. It takes 8 minutes for sunlight to reach Earth.

Radio waves travel at the speed of light, so when communicating from Earth with probes and rovers on Mars, there is always a slight delay whose length depends on the current separation between the planets. When controllers send a signal or command to Mars, they have to wait double the time for a response to return.

At closest distances it only takes about three or four minutes for a signal to reach Mars, but when Mars' orbit takes it far away it can take nearly a half hour each way. But if Mars is on the other side of the Sun, communication will black out completely until it passes into view again.

30. MARINER 4: THE TRAILBLAZER

NASA began sending out deep space probes in the 1960's when advances in rocket technology made it possible. The Mariner program was established to send probes to visit and collect data from the Moon and the interior planets Mercury, Venus, and Mars.

The Mariner craft were small robotic probes with solar panels, scientific instruments, and (on some missions) cameras. A few of the Mariner missions either flew by or entered orbit around Mars, collecting data and photographs that revolutionized our understanding of the planet.

In 1965 Mariner 4 was the first space probe to successfully pass by Mars and transmit observations back to Earth. It included the first close-up photographs of the surface of Mars, giving us our first glimpse of the terrain of another world. Mariner 6 and 7 returned four years later for another successful pass, and Mariner 9, in 1971, became the first probe to orbit Mars.

31. THE VIKING LANDER

During the 1960's and 1970's, the United States and the Soviet Union were locked in a tight race to reach Mars with space probes. Both nations had a mixture of successes and failures. There were several lost or crashed probes, but several missions were successful at gathering photographs and instrument data by passing close by Mars or achieving brief orbit around the planet. The ultimate goal, though, was to land on the surface.

On May 28, 1971, the Soviets were the first to safely land a probe on the surface of Mars without crashing, but their Mars 3 lander stopped transmitting just a few seconds after touching down and failed to collect any meaninful data.

Finally, on July 20, 1976, The United States successfully landed its Viking 1 probe on the surface of Mars. An orbiter was left above to help Viking relay data back to Earth. The probe remained active for six years before losing contact. It sent back stunning photographs of the Martian surface along with data from multiple scientific instruments that gave scientists their first glimpses of what Mars is like.

32. BEAGLE 2 – THE BRITISH INVASION

The United States and the Soviet Union (and later Russia) have dominated space exploration through most of the space age. But Europe gradually entered the fray with the creation of the European Space Agency (ESA) in the 1970's.

In 2003, the ESA launched Mars Express to conduct research on Mars' capacity to support life and the chemistry of its geological composition. The Mars Express orbiter itself conducted surveys of the planet using specialized antennas, but it also deployed a surface lander called Beagle 2.

Developed by the British, Beagle 2, was named in honor of the ship HMS Beagle which carried naturalist Charles Darwin on his famous journeys. The landing probe was designed to dig into the surface of Mars looking for signs of past microscopic life.

Unfortunately, contact with Beagle 2 was lost and its fate wasn't learned until the Mars Reconnaissance Orbiter found it in surface images taken in 2015. The craft appeared to have landed safely, but incomplete deployment of its solar panels likely contributed to its falure.

33. THE MARS PHOENIX LANDER (AND INTERPLANETARY DVD DELIVERY SERVICE)

The search for water on Mars and the assessment of its future human habitability have become increasingly high priorities for Mars missions in recent decades. NASA and JPL launched the Phoenix probe, which landed in 2008, to study those prospects.

Phoenix became the first craft to land in one of the polar regions of Mars. The solar-powered lander was equipped with a robotic arm for digging a couple of feet into the surface for the sampling of dirt and ice. Several sophisticated instruments on board, including microscopes, analyzed the chemistry and composition of the samples and transmitted results back to Earth. Meteorological instruments collected additional data about Mars' atmosphere and weather. There was also an imager with dual cameras for taking high-definition stereo images of the surface. The successful mission collected a great deal of useful information, even exceeding its planned timeline, but finally lost power after a cold winter.

An interesting part of the Phoenix payload was a DVD containing digitized books and audio related to Mars, including the infamous 1958 The War of the Worlds radio broadcast. Millions of Mars enthusiasts had their names included in a list on the DVD, for reading by future visitors.

34. THE MARS RECONNAISSANCE ORBITER

Before attempting the difficult task of landing a craft or probe on another planet or moon, quite a bit of preliminary work must be done. As much as possible must be understood about the landing surface and the conditions of the destination.

In 2005, NASA launched the Mars Reconnaissance Orbiter to study the climate and geological features of Mars both to learn more about the planet and to help select suitable areas on the surface for future landing missions. To date, the satellite is still operational in orbit around Mars and has relayed valuable data back to Earth.

The orbiter has been instrumental in identifying informative features on the surface of Mars, including the location of water ice, and even some narrow seasonal channels of salty liquid water on mountain slopes.

35. MARS ARTIFICIAL SATELLITES

Earth's orbit is starting to get a little crowded. Between scientific, communication, and military satellites there are an estimated 6,000 pieces of man-made machinery in orbit – most of which are no longer functioning. Although Mars doesn't hold a candle to Earth, it's amassing quite a collection of satellites on its own.

Aside from its two small moons, there are currently 16 satellites in orbit around Mars. A few of the spacecraft, like the Soviet Mars, and Phobos 2 orbiters, and NASA's Viking and Mariner 9, lost contact decades ago and are circling in quiet retirement. The Mars Global Surveyor, which lost radio contact in 2006 is also still in orbit.

But there are eight functioning satellites in orbit around Mars from a variety of space agencies around the world including NASA, the ESA, Russia, India, China, and the United Arab Emirates. Eventually, the orbit of the older, non-functioning satellites will degrade and they'll either burn up in the atmosphere or crash land. With missions to Mars ramping up, however, there are plenty on the way to take their place.

36. FAILED MARS MISSIONS – AN OPPORTUNITY TO LEARN

Man has been trying reach Mars, one of our most intriguing neighbors, since the Space Age began. To date there have been nearly fifty missions to Mars, including fly-by probes, orbiters, landers, and rovers. But not all of these missions have been successful. In fact, a few have quite literally crashed and burned.

Only about half of all Mars missions have completed their missions throughout history so far, although many are still ongoing and performing well. Missions have failed for different reasons – loss of communication, faulty equipment, and design flaws have been common culprits. Some probes are lost in space, some burned up in the Martian atmosphere, some crash landed on the surface, and some landed safely but the failed shortly afterward.

Despite the expense and embarrassment of some of the spectacular failures of missions to Mars, each and every attempt provided valuable lessons for future endeavors. Scientists and engineers have learned from past mistakes and unforseen circumstances to get better and better at getting to Mars. In space travel, we can learn as much from failure as we can in success.

37. MARS CLIMATE ORBITER - THE $327 MILLION DOLLAR MISTAKE

How many feet are in a meter? How many kilograms in a pound? How many quarts in a liter? Conversion between different measurement systems is a common exercise in school. But what if it wasn't a science exam at stake, but rather a nearly multi-million-dollar space mission?

In the late 1990's NASA developed a Mars satellite in conjunction with the Lockheed Martin aerospace corporation. The purpose of the Mars Climate Orbiter was to study the climate and atmosphere of Mars. The orbiter launched in December 1998, but nine months later it lost contact when trying to achieve orbit around Mars.

The failure of the mission was traced back to a simple unit conversion problem. Lockheed had provided software specifications to NASA using

English (feet, pounds, ounces, etc.) units. NASA, however, uses metric-based units like meters, kilograms, and liters. The proper protocols weren't followed to check the units, so the trajectory of the spacecraft was wrong.

The total cost of the mission was about $327 million, making it one of the most expensive math errors in history.

38. MARS PATHFINDER

The 1996 Mars Pathfinder mission was a milestone achievement in planetary exploration. The objective of Pathfinder was to land a "base station" on the surface of Mars and deploy a small robotic rover, named Sojourner, to explore a small area around the landing site.

The purposes of Pathfinder were to test a new type of airbag system for safe landing on Mars, to test the feasibility of controlling robotic rovers with onboard obstacle avoidance capabilities, and if possible, to gather photographs and data about the Martian soil, terrain, and climate.

The mission was largely a success and set the stage for future surface missions and rovers.

Unfortunately, the Pathfinder base station lost radio contact with Earth (possibly due to a battery failure), stranding the rover in the middle of a study.

39. SOJOURNER: THE LOST TRAVELER

The 1996 Mars Pathfinder mission, among its many other purposes, was conceived to help test the process of deploying a robot rover on the surface of Mars. The small six-wheeled rover, named Sojourner, weighed just 25 lbs. When it rolled off the Pathfinder lander it was the first wheeled vehicle to operate on another planet (there were manned moon "buggies" during the Apollo missions).

Sojourner, like the rovers that succeeded it, was solar powered and featured cameras along with several scientific instrument. Although it was only designed for a 1-week mission, it continued gathering data for three months until its signal from the Pathfinder base station was lost. Its last known location was about 100 m from the Pathfinder landing site.

Although Sojourner was no longer communicating, it may have still been carrying on operations on its own after the signal was lost, so there's no way to know its location until it's found by future rovers, aerial photographs, or visitors.

40. THE MOST EXPENSIVE JUNKYARD IN THE SOLAR SYSTEM

When humans eventually land on Mars, possibly within the next 10-15 years, they will find more than just a bunch of rocks and red dirt. They have been preceded by dozens of prior missions many of which were landers and rovers that are still operational on the Martian surface. They may encounter some that have run out of power, been overcome but dust storms, or just plain failed.

They may also come across the debris of some of the more explosive failures of past missions to Mars. The Soviet Mars 2 vehicle crashed into the surface of Mars in 1972 in a failed attempt to safely land. Its identical partner, Mars 3, successfully landed but died shortly after. In 1999, the Mars Polar Lander, sent to help study the Martian Climate, vanished into the atmosphere, and eventually impacted on the ground.

Between the crash debris and several lost or dead pieces of expensive high-tech machinery, when astronauts arrive on Mars, they may have some cleaning up to do.

41. CURIOSITY – THE MARTIAN WORKHORSE

One of the most successful, productive, and longest-lasting missions to Mars has been that of the Curiosity rover.

Curiosity launched from Earth in late November 2011 and successfully touched down on Mars just over eight months later. Curiosity's mission was to investigate the geological and climatic history of Mars to determine whether its past conditions could have supported life – specifically microscopic life. It's about the size of a car, has six wheels, and has multiple scientific instruments and cameras.

Curiosity successfully completed its main objectives, helping scientists conclude that microbes could have existed on ancient Mars. But since Curiosity remained online and operational, NASA decided to extend its mission and give it more to do. It has been working ever since, sending data and photographs back to Earth to help us better understand the environment of Mars.

Since Curiosity has been so durable and useful for many years, its design has been used to develop more rovers for present and future missions.

42. INSIGHT: A PLANETARY "SONOGRAM"

Interior Exploration using Seismic Investigations, Geodesy and Heat Transport. Now that's a mouthful. You can understand why NASA refers to this mission as InSight for short. The InSight probe launched, after a two-year delay in its original schedule, in the spring of 2018, landing on the Martian surface in late November of the same year.

InSight was equipped with seismological and thermal instruments designed to study the interior structure of Mars. Data will be used to construct 3D models of the interior of the planet to give scientists clues about its geological past, present, and future. This information is also expected to shed light on the formation and evolution of the other planets in the solar system, including Earth.

43. MARS PERSEVERANCE

The Mars Perseverance rover is the most recent mission to Mars and its media visibility has captured the imaginations of people all over the world. Perseverence launched from Earth in July of 2020 as part of a multi-faceted mission.

Perseverance took its design from a previous mission vehicle, the Curiosity Rover, which has done very well on Mars and is still operational. It is car-sized, has six wheels, and boasts some of the most sophisticated scientific instruments available. It is also equipped with high-definition cameras that have returned stunning images of Mars.

In addition to supporting the objective of its predecessor, Curiosity, to study the past environment of Mars, Perseverance is also tasked with looking for evidence that microscopic life may have previously existed on the planet. It also will collect rock and soil samples and investigate whether oxygen can be obtained from the atmosphere for future human missions.

Inside the belly of Perseverance is a small helicopter-like drone that will be deployed to take aerial images.

44. INGENUITY – TAKING DRONES TO A NEW LEVEL

The Mars 2020 mission that launched the iconic Perseverance rover included a small stowaway named Ingenuity. Ingenuity is a helicopter drone that is stored in a small compartment on the underside of the Perseverance rover. It will attempt to become the first flight of a vehicle within the atmosphere of a planet other than Earth.

Ingenuity's body consists of a small rectangular case, about the size of a shoe box. It has two rotors, each four feet in diameter, that counter-rotate on a single axis. Underneath are four spindly landing legs. The drone has a small solar panel on top to charge its batteries and is equipped with cameras and navigational sensors.

The initial mission of Ingenuity is simple – to demonstrate the feasibility of flying in the Martian atmosphere. After the Perseverance rover drops it off in a suitable location it will attempt to take off, conduct a short flight, land safely, and make history.

45. FUTURE MISSIONS

Mars has been a focal point of space agencies across the world in recent years, including NASA, The ESA, and groups from Russia, Japan, India, China, and the United Arab Emirates. The interest in Mars is centered around both learning about the formation and history of our solar system (including whether life has existed outside of Earth) and the future of human exploration of space.

Most planned missions for the near future consist of additional orbiters for communications and atmospheric study, as well as some "fly-by" missions by probes that are heading toward outer planets for other objectives. There will also be some more surface-landing missions to collect samples and to prepare for future human missions.

Current plans to land humans safely on the surface of Mars involve both public and private agencies. The SpaceX corporation is currently developing a reusable landing vehicle that it hopes will allow them to have a manned mission by 2026.

46. SPACEX: PRIVATE PIONEERS

In the earliest years of the Space Age , the only entities capable of taking on the risk and expense of space exploration were governments. The United States and the Soviet Union led the charge beginning in the 1950's with dedicated space agencies. As we learned more about space travel, and technology improved, it became feasible for private companies to start launching their own space-bound ventures.

One such company is SpaceX, the Space Exploration Technologies Corporation, which was founded by the CEO of the electric vehicle company, Tesla. SpaceX was formed with the specific purpose of reducing the cost of space travel in order to make manned missions and the eventual colonization of Mars a reality.

The SpaceX Starship project is the ongoing development of a reusable rocket that can take off from the Earth, land on another moon or planet, and return. The company hopes to land humans on Mars by 2026.

47. GETTING PEOPLE TO MARS

Because of the differing orbits of Earth and Mars, they only pass reasonably close to each other a little more than every 2 years. We try to use these short windows of opportunity to launch rockets to Mars with minimum travel time, which is about seven to nine months with current technology.

Humans have lived in space, on the International Space Station, for as many as 340 days – more than enough time to make it to Mars. But when you factor in the mission time, the round trip, and the time waiting for the best return launch window, a manned Mars mission would expose humans to the hazards and radiation of space (not to mention the inhospitable conditions of Mars itself) for at least a year and a half.

This would make it the longest and most dangerous human space mission ever attempted. When a manned mission to Mars is ever attempted in will be a monumental achievement of human ingenuity and bravery.

48. NASA FUTURE MANNED MISSIONS

Estimates put the cost of sending humans to Mars at roughly one half trillion US dollars. That's one of the biggest reasons that such a mission has yet to occur. Nevertheless, long-term plans are in place by both private and government entities to land people on the Red Planet.

NASA is taking a step-by-step approach, with plans to prepare for a future manned Mars mission by first returning humans to the Moon. After learning more about the effect extended periods of time on the surface of another body, NASA hopes to leverage the lessons of establishing a permanent human presence on the Moon to plan a safe and productive human journey to Mars.

Before trying to set foot on Mars, though, the challenge of getting there will be addressed. Current US government directives call for sending astronauts to orbit Mars and return to Earth by the mid-2030's.

49. TERRAFORMING MARS?

When astronauts go to space, or walk on the Moon, they take a bit of the Earth with them. Shielded and pressurized capsules and suits simulate the atmosphere of Earth to keep human explorers alive. But what if instead of living in little self-contained environments like goldfish in a bowl, we could transform an entire planet into a livable habitat?

Terraforming is the (theoretical) process of creating an Earth-like atmosphere and environment on an otherwise uninhabitable planet or Moon. Because of the location of Mars, its general similarities to Earth, and the presence of water, it has been suggested as a possible candidate for terraforming in the far future.

Despite the positive features of Mars with respect to terraforming, though, it poses many challenges. Its low gravity can't hold a thick atmosphere and its lack of a strong magnetic field subjects it to dangerous doses of radiation. Even if technological advancements make terraforming Mars feasible, it could take hundreds or even thousands of years to complete the process.

Nevertheless, multiple methods for terraforming Mars are being studies, and will be updated the more we learn about the planet.

50. MARS: HOME SWEET HOME?

The 1969 Apollo 11 Moon landing is still one of the greatest achievements of mankind. It was an improbable feat – and everything had to go off without a hitch to pull it off. The eyes of the world were glued to their TV screens as live footage of the first people to walk on another world was broadcast through space.

As difficult as it is to get humans safely to the Moon and back, doing so on Mars will take a monumental effort. Mars is much further away, and if something goes wrong (like it did with the aborted Apollo 13 Moon mission), astronauts won't be able to just easily turn around and come home. Landing on Mars will be more difficult than on the Moon because of its atmosphere and higher gravity.

So, why go to Mars? Right now, Earth is all we have. We know that asteroids have wiped out entire generations of previous species on Earth (like the dinosaurs) and could do the same to us. We know millions of years from now the Sun will swell in size and make the Earth unsuitable for life. We know our population is continuing to grow, consuming more resources and space. We'll eventually need somewhere else to go.

Despite the danger, expense, and technical challenges, it is in the best interest of humanity to visit and eventually colonize other planets. Mars is the closest, most suitable candidate. It could be the future home of mankind.

OTHER RESOURCES:

Mars Overview

https://solarsystem.nasa.gov/planets/mars/overvie
w/

All About Mars https://mars.nasa.gov/all-about-
mars/facts/

Mars Missions https://mars.nasa.gov/

READ OTHER
50 THINGS TO KNOW
BOOKS

50 Things to Know

Stay up to date with new releases on Amazon:

https://amzn.to/2VPNGr7

CZYKPublishing.com

50 Things to Know

We'd love to hear what you think about our content! Please leave your honest review of this book on Amazon and Goodreads. We appreciate your positive and constructive feedback. Thank you.

Made in the USA
Middletown, DE
13 July 2021

44128679R00044